GOLDWORK

GOLDWORK

Valerie Campbell-Harding

Jane Lemon

Kit Pyman

SEARCH PRESS

First published in Great Britain 1995.

Search Press Limited
Wellwood, North Farm Road,
Tunbridge Wells, Kent, TN2 3DR

Copyright © Search Press Ltd. 1995

This edition contains material from *Goldwork,* originally published in 1983, and from *The Madeira Book of Gold and Silver Embroidery*, published in 1987, as well as new material.

Photographs by Search Press Studios.

ISBN 0 85532 778 2

Printed in Malaysia

List of contributors

Allison Blair
Valerie Campbell-Harding
Jean Brown
Mollie Collins
Vera Dawson
Sylvia Drinkwater
Elizabeth Elvin
Diana Gill
Belinda Hill
Heidi Jenkins
Jane Lemon
Jan Messent
Tryphena Orchard
Jean Panter
Jennie Parry
Eileen Plumbridge
Kit Pyman
Dorothy Reglar
Angela Thompson
May Williams

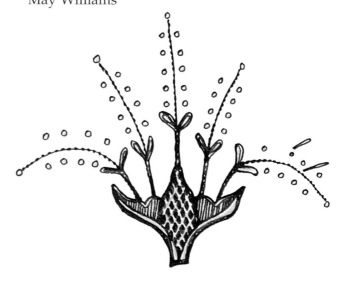

ABOVE
Typical small motif used for powdering: diaper silk and gold with couched gold and spangles.

OPPOSITE
Belt-buckle, *by Belinda Hill: a design in padded gold kid and gold threads, worked on a brown silk background, with an edging of pearl purl.*

Contents

Introduction: the history of goldwork

Throughout history gold has been a symbol of wealth, power, and status, and metal-thread embroidery has always enhanced the rich fabrics that proclaim these desirable attributes. Gold, one of the first metals to be discovered and used by early man, is treasured for its value, beauty and malleability: it was originally associated with myth and magic, and with the worship of the sun. Ownership of golden artefacts bestowed magic powers – in ancient myth the apples of the Hesperides were made of pure gold and, even centuries later, a design of apples in gilded thread was embroidered on the cloak of the King of Mercia to bring him good fortune.

Homer relates the story that Helen of Troy's golden spindle could produce only perfect thread, and the myth of the Golden Fleece remained potent for centuries, entwined with the mystique of kingship in the western world.

The first gold threads were exactly that – strands of pure beaten gold – cut in narrow strips from the flattened metal. Gold spangles and hammered gold cut into shapes were also used from a very early date, and examples have been found stitched into the felted fabric preserved in ancient Scythian tombs.

Silver never seems to have had quite the same appeal, perhaps because of its tendency to tarnish; however, once the technique for bonding gold to silver became known, most 'gold' threads were actually gilded silver strips wrapped around a core of silk, parchment, animal gut, or paper.

Wrapped thread required skill in manipulation, and techniques were devised for couching it down and laying the threads at angles to catch the light. With the development of wire drawing, silver wire could be coated with gold to make a very fine round thread. This could then be beaten flat, and later the spiral springs of purls, twisted gold and silver thread, and metallised plaits and braids added to the heavy texture of this type of embroidery.

Like so many other arts, embroidery with metal threads came from the east. The Egyptians, Assyrians and Babylonians have left descriptions of their gilded textiles, and in the Bible the Old Testament described how 'they did beat the gold into thin plates and cut it into wires to work it in the blue and in the purple and in the scarlet and in the fine linen with cunning work', while the Psalmist sings of a bride wearing 'clothing of wrought gold'. It seems likely that this was woven rather than

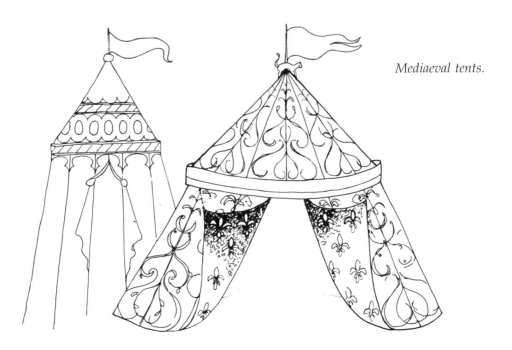

Mediaeval tents.

embroidered, and it is interesting in the context to note the extraordinarily lavish use of metal as a textile; when the tomb of the Empress Honorius, who died in AD400, was opened in 1544 she was found to be shrouded in layers of cloth-of-gold, which melted down into 16kg (36lb) of pure metal.

Threads and woven textiles travelled to the west in the silk caravans across Central Asia, providing the rich clothing of the Greeks and Romans. Pliny talks of gold 'spun or woven like wool, without any wool being mixed with it', and describes a kind of bullion work – an example of which was discovered recently at an archaeological site at Kostolats – reminding us that edicts had to be issued against the excessive luxury of Roman dress.

The main distribution centres for textiles, and metal and silk threads, were originally Tyre and what is now Beirut, lying at the western end of the caravan routes. However, once the carefully guarded secrets of silk-making were smuggled to the West, the manufacture and weaving of silk ceased to be a Chinese monopoly and was practised by the Byzantines, who made it an Imperial monopoly in their turn and who carefully controlled all related industries; gold-embroiderers were among the craftsmen permanently employed in the Imperial palace.

In pre-industrial days, embroidery was a professional skill as well as an organised domestic activity. Much of the commercial work was done by men, and workshops and guilds existed to satisfy the considerable demand for elaborately decorated hangings, furnishings, trappings, tents, and garments. Characteristic Byzantine designs consisted of elaborate patterning with figures worked in laid gold, shown up against a brilliantly coloured silk background. The tones of the gold were varied by couching it in minutely different directions so as to catch the light, rather in the way the pieces are laid in the famous Ravenna mosaics.

After the conversion of Constantine the Great to Christianity, the manufacture of ecclesiastical textiles and furnishing became an important export industry and remained so for the next thousand years. Embroidered fabrics were used not only for vestments and altars, but also for walls, arcades and doors. In the seventh century it was said that the whole nave of St Denis in Paris was hung with gold-embroidered fabrics set with pearls. These were almost certainly made in Constantinople.

In time this 'second Rome' declined sufficiently to allow serious competition. Metal threads could be obtained from places like Venice, Cyprus and Palermo, and the use of embroidered textiles spread to all the smaller churches of the West. However, the Turkish conquerors of Constantinople in their turn had an equal appreciation of the glories of metal-thread work, and subsequently evolved a form of embroidered apparel which became the traditional court dress of the Balkans. Echoes of this can be found in the goldwork embroidery on peasant costume to this day.

To date, the earliest surviving example of English metal-thread work is the tenth-century stole and maniple of St Cuthbert from Durham Cathedral.

Part of St Cuthbert's maniple.

This shows the influence of Byzantine design in the disposition of the figures and in the elaborate lettering, but it is executed in the indigenous manner – that is to say, the figures are embroidered in coloured silks touched with gold, and the background is entirely covered with laid gold. This is couched approximately five threads to the millimetre (125 to the inch) with superb mastery of an exacting technique and is one of the few pieces to survive which is worked in the pure metal. The handling of gold thread seems to have been a long tradition in Anglo-Saxon history. This resulted in the work which became famous all over Europe in the Middle Ages as, *opus anglicanum*. One characteristic of this 'English work' was the use of underside couching, which enabled large areas of fabric to be closely covered with gold thread while remaining pliable. A possible reason for the adoption of the technique was the requirement for a rich background to the figures, in the absence of the magnificent woven silks used in Constantinople.

The splendid fabrics and embroideries of the east were brought home by returning crusaders and must have opened a new world to the workshops of Europe. The rise of heraldic devices necessitated by the increasing use of armour offered a great field for decoration: friend was distinguished from foe on the battlefield and in the jousts by the colour and brilliance of the devices worked in bright silks and gold threads. The widespread use of public display as political and economic strategies promoted the manufacture of costly regalia and portable furnishings of great splendour.

Contemporary descriptions of the Field of Cloth of Gold (1517), so called because of the lavish use of that textile in costume, tents and hangings, give some idea of the glory of that last meeting of undivided Christendom: intended as a meeting to establish friendship between the two nations, it virtually became an international display of one-upmanship. It was remarked later that many of those attending wore their mills, their forests and their meadows on their shoulders, and for some of them the weight of the metal thread on the clothing must have equalled a weight of debt which took a lifetime to repay. The vestments and hangings were equally magnificent. One cope was described as gold tissue 'pricked' with fine gold and embroidered with pearls and precious stones, and a pavilion was listed in the accounts as being lined with blue velvet which was powdered with 72,544 fleur-de-lys worked in gold thread!

The decline of heraldry and the rise of the reformed Church reduced opportunities for the lavish display of gold embroidery, although metal-thread work was used on costume until the eighteenth century. Very little early work has survived, which is hardly surprising when the value of the materials is considered; indeed, the wealth of precious metals, pearls and jewels on some pieces must have ensured their subsequent destruction.

A large amount of ecclesiastical embroidery was destroyed or cut up for secular use during the Reformation, and at a later date it is recorded that a hanging in Canterbury Cathedral was burnt to reclaim the gold.

However, metal rarely vanishes, it only metamorphoses; and it is interesting to reflect that nearly all the gold which has ever been mined is still around in some form or another. The goldwork described by Homer on the mantle of Odysseus may have been melted down and hammered into an antique coin, and the scavenged epaulettes of the grandee transmuted into a piece of Victorian jewellery.

Metal-thread embroidery on costume survived almost to the end of the eighteenth century; a royal court was still a glittering affair and brilliant orders and decorations were worn on formal occasions. However, the fashion for English country life and the emergence of the soberly clad business entrepreneur began to replace the silks of the Age of Reason with the broadcloth of the age of industry; a process much hastened by the French Revolution, which eventually swept the extravagance of gold and silver from the dress of most prudent men.

Traditional design in couched silver braid on peasant costume.

Goldwork today

Whereas metal-thread work was once an outward expression of temporal power and spiritual glory, now there are other ways of conveying different messages, and the only vestiges left on costume are badges of rank and braiding on dress uniforms. Beautiful vestments and church furnishings are still being made, but the content of precious metal is low, and the effect is produced as much by colour and design as by costly materials.

The light has changed, too. The flat lighting prevailing now does not call forth the same golden brilliance that was reflected in the flickering light of candles, bringing life to the scenes so vividly displayed to an illiterate congregation.

Threads also have changed. All that glisters is hardly ever gold; rather it is metallised rayon or some gilded man-made fibre, and there is a variety of sparkling threads available now that the ancient world could never have imagined.

Materials for goldwork today include all kinds of shining embroidery threads, plus knitting and crochet threads with metallised effects and the new glittering threads for machine embroidery. Added to these are cords and braids, gilded leather, and a vast range of beads, jewels and stones.

The fascination of this embroidery lies in the rich effects achieved by metal threads where the direction of the threads and the play of light alter the tone, and make the surface appear to lie on different planes.

Church work has traditionally been executed in the most costly and rare materials, but today the value of the work often lies more in the excellence of the design. The chapter in this book on designing for the Church provides useful guidelines, and is illustrated by a description of the execution of a commission for an altar frontal from the original conception to the final placement.

Metal-thread work is still a viable technique today, but whereas the true metal still costs a great deal and requires a skilful technique for application, the new man-made gold and silver threads are vastly malleable and versatile and easy to use (some may even be washed and ironed). This book illustrates many ideas for new applications of this historic and beautiful craft.

Dragon with pearl, by Sylvia Drinkwater, in modern materials: couched braids, cords, beads, sequins, padded gilded leather and imitation Jap gold on a pure-silk dupion fabric.

Goldwork techniques

Development of metal threads

Metal 'thread' for embroidery has always been subject to technical improvement, mostly in order to reduce the cost, and the different types of thread have inevitably brought about changes in their use.

As soon as the technique of bonding gold over silver was discovered, the original pure beaten gold flat strip developed into gilded silver strip. Gilded silver could also be drawn into wire, and this also was beaten flat and spiralled around a core.

Such heavy and costly thread was laid on the surface of a fabric and held down with silk. These couching stitches were exactly spaced and formed regular diaper patterns, adding much interest to the work. In underside couching, a strong linen thread pulled tiny loops of the gold thread through to the back, leaving dimples on the front which divided the golden surface into facets.

This early type of metal thread had enhanced the garb of mediaeval people in small ways as well as on the great occasions; stiff bands of embroidery bordered their gowns, shoes were covered with gold mesh, and plaits were encased in long silken tubes ornamented with gold and silver cord.

In the sixteenth century a great technical advance, the invention of the steel draw-plate, made possible the production of fine wires of regular diameter. This led to the development of silver-gilt passing threads which could be stitched through a fabric, and which eventually evolved into silver and gold lace. When the fine wires were beaten out, they could be made into the finest and lightest wrapped 'sewing gold' with an orange silk core.

The springy 'purl', which came in many sizes and textures and consisted of the finest wire twisted to form a tube, could be cut up and applied like a bead, or coiled into circles or loops. Although most purl was the familiar silver-gilt, silk purl was also made. This consisted of tarnishable copper wire wrapped with silk and then coiled; it was a cheaper version which was applied to objects where constant handling might spoil the fabric, and where a great deal of purl was required.

As a result of these innovations, couching became more elaborate and rose into three dimensions – threads being couched over string, paper, padding and chamois leather. Purl introduced a new heavy texture. At the other extreme, fine goldwork could be done in 'passing' thread on delicate fabrics, and designs could be worked in metal threads in techniques other than couching.

Gold combined with colourful silk remained a perennial favourite: bright flowers appear with coiling stems of gold in plaited braid stitches; canvaswork 'sprigs' in tiny stitches are worked or outlined with gold; single blooms shine from the gauntlets of ceremonial gloves, coiled with metal-thread, trimmed with gold lace and powdered with seed pearls.

Stumpwork, an interesting seventeenth-century three-dimensional technique, used buttonhole stitch to form the fine metal thread into tiny garments and canopies, and the panel itself might be framed with bullion. Bullion was a very heavy type of purl, and 'bullion knots' resemble a short length of bullion lying on the surface of the fabric.

In the eighteenth century metal threads were combined with quilting for cushions, bed-covers and petticoats. Made of silk or fine linen, they were quilted in a diaper pattern and embroidered with sprays of flowers in coloured silks held in golden bows or baskets: some of the quilting patterns were imitated in couched gold thread. Men's coats and waistcoats were commonly embroidered in silk and metal threads and chenille.

The light style of the eighteenth century deteriorated in the mid nineteenth century into heavy metal-thread work upon velvet backgrounds, used on smoking caps, cushions, bags, lamp mats and even tea-cosies. However, by the end of the century, the introduction of 'Japanese' gold, which was silvered and gilded paper wrapped around a core, made the thread lighter and cheaper, and embroidered hangings by William Morris show delicate designs merely touched with gold. The Art needlework of the early twentieth century employed metal threads merely for outline or emphasis.

A great revival in Church embroidery since the Second World War, led by Beryl Dean, has exploited the potential of the newly introduced threads and materials – a study of her work is a revelation in the art of using metal threads, gilded kid, PVC, coloured purls and many other materials.

Apart from ecclesiastical work, traditional metal-thread work is today practised mostly in the third world on such items as evening bags, wallets and waistcoats, which are sold rather as 'ethnic' products than as everyday wear. However, this book shows how gold can be combined with other techniques in most beautiful and interesting ways, and that we have by no means come to the end of a technique which has been a delight to mankind ever since the discovery of precious metals.

BELOW
Samples of metal threads in general use. The threads shown are available in different sizes in gold and silver, and some of them also in copper.

Design

Any type of design is suitable for metal-thread embroidery, because it is an adaptable technique which suits both geometric and free-flowing designs. Nowadays metal threads are combined with coloured stitchery, often only occupying a small part of the whole. However, one must be careful to give this considered thought and not just throw on a few gold threads: 'cheap and quick' metal-thread work is unattractive.

Aim for simplicity and richness. When designing for clothes and vestments, which should hang softly and drape well, beware of using too much metal-thread work: it can make the fabric heavy and stiff.

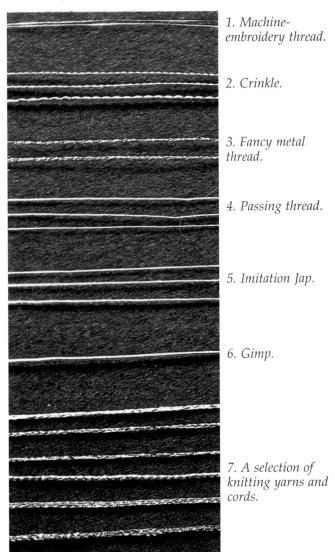

1. Machine-embroidery thread.

2. Crinkle.

3. Fancy metal thread.

4. Passing thread.

5. Imitation Jap.

6. Gimp.

7. A selection of knitting yarns and cords.

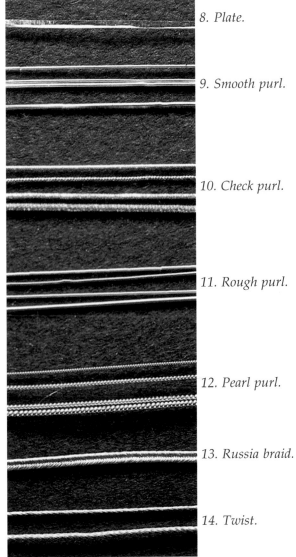

8. Plate.

9. Smooth purl.

10. Check purl.

11. Rough purl.

12. Pearl purl.

13. Russia braid.

14. Twist.

Fabrics

Because the threads are fairly heavy, the ground fabric should be strong and closely woven. This is backed, if necessary, with a cotton or linen fabric to support the weight and avoid puckering. Silks look beautiful with metal threads, for the sheen acts as a foil to them, but they are expensive. Substitutes may often be found among furnishing fabrics – including man-made fabrics if the quality is good enough – and even scrim and organza can be used as long as the finest threads are used with them.

Try to avoid brocades, damasks and patterned fabrics, which vie for attention with the embroidery.

Fabrics unsuitable for work solely with metal threads can be used as appliqué within the design.

Sewing threads

Twisted sewing silk or transparent nylon threads are suitable for couching metal threads and should be gold, grey or rust to match them. Fine embroidery threads of any sort can give added colour.

Metal threads

Real gold was used for centuries in metal-thread work, but today most of the threads are imitation. There is such a wide range that only the most readily available kinds are mentioned here; a selection is shown on page 11. Some will not pass through the fabric and are used only in couching, while others can be threaded through a needle.

There are many different types, such as 'twist', 'crinkle', 'tambour', 'passing' and 'gimp', made in different colours and thicknesses. There are metallic cords, and braids both fine and thick, and a flat ribbon-like strip called 'plate' which is very stiff and shiny.

There is also a group of coiled wires, called 'purls', of various textures, which are cut into short lengths and sewn on like beads, or couched down. There is a thread called 'imitation Jap', which is made by wrapping very fine gold- or silver-coloured paper around a core of threads. This is inexpensive and is often used for couching.

Finally, there are the metallic yarns and mixtures which are sold for knitting and crochet. You will probably wish to build up your stock gradually, and there is no need to buy the real gold threads until you are more experienced at this type of embroidery.

Other equipment

Frame Types of frames and methods of stretching fabric over them are described on pages 14–16.

Thimble A thimble is needed for accurate sewing. Sometimes a second one is worn on the middle finger of the other hand.

Needles Crewel needles sizes 8 and 10 can be used for most of the sewing. A large chenille needle is required for taking ends through to the back.

Scissors You will need an old pair of straight nail-scissors for cutting the tough wires and threads, a small pair of embroidery scissors for cutting the sewing threads, and a good pair of dressmaking shears for the fabrics.

Tweezers These are useful for picking up beads and short lengths of wire or purls.

Stiletto Use a stiletto or awl to make holes in the fabric to take the ends of thick cords or threads.

Cutting boards A piece of stiff felt-covered card about 15cm (6in) square can be used when cutting purl. It prevents the tiny pieces from jumping about.

Felt This is required for padding. Use yellow for gold and grey for silver.

String This is also used for padding. It can be dyed by dipping it into yellow drawing ink, so that it will be less noticeable between gaps in the threads.

Leathers Gold and silver kid are often used in this type of embroidery. As they are dominant, and readily catch the eye, it is best to use them in small quantities.

Beeswax Beeswax is used to strengthen the sewing thread, and helps to eliminate twisting and friction. It can be bought in special containers through which the thread can be pulled to coat it with wax.

Plastic boxes Boxes with transparent lids, such as fishermen use to store flies, are ideal for storing metal threads. Alternatively, they can be wrapped in tissue paper and kept in cardboard boxes. Do not keep metal threads in polythene bags as some of them will tarnish.

Sea-chest, *a goldwork box by Diana Gill. The box is covered in turquoise linen embroidered with designs of seashells worked in gold and silver threads and gold kid.*

Gold beaded belt, *by Dorothy Reglar. This belt is entirely covered with a rich assortment of gold beads and sequins, with a decorative edge.*

Goldwork equipment: *a collection of the beads, threads and tools used for the technique of goldwork.*

Framing up

All metal-thread embroidery should be done on a frame. The frame supports the fabric and leaves both hands free for the actual stitchery, and the fabric (or the backing fabric) is kept drum-taut. A frame also keeps the fabric at the correct tension, particularly important with this type of embroidery because it is never stretched afterwards, as damp tarnishes the threads. The frame can be a commercial slate frame, an old picture frame, a home-made frame, or a ring frame.

Methods of stretching fabric – which is called 'framing up' – on different kinds of frames are described below.

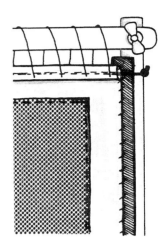

A corner of a slate frame showing the back fabric stitched to the tape on the round bar, and laced to the flat bar.

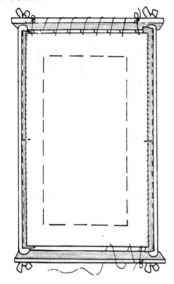

A slate frame, with the fabric in the process of being framed up.

Commercial slate frame

1. Cut the fabric about the size of the frame (which must be larger than the finished design).

2. Mark the centre of the webbing on the rollers.

3. Mark centre top and bottom of fabric.

4. Fold under a small hem at the top of the fabric, match to centre of webbing, pin, then oversew from the centre outwards.

5. Repeat with other end of fabric and other roller.

6. Turn under a hem each side of the fabric over a length of string, and tack. Assemble frame.

7. Using crochet cotton, lace the sides of the fabric over the arms of the frame. Tie the ends at each corner.

8. Tighten the frame until the fabric is evenly tensioned.

Home-made frame

A frame can be made of four pieces of wood about 2.5cm (1in) square, joined at the corners. Alternatively, an old picture frame can be used if it is soft enough to take drawing pins (thumbtacks) or tacks; or an artists' stretcher frame can be made up from lengths bought at a artists' supplier. The fabric is framed up by being pinned, tacked or stapled around the outer edge of the frame as follows:

1. Mark the centre of each side of the frame.

2. Cut the fabric about 10cm (4in) larger all round than the frame.

3. Mark the centre of each side of the fabric.

4. Match the centre fabric sides to the centre frame sides, and fix each centre side with a pin or staple.

5. Pin outwards from each centre towards the corner, tensioning the fabric as you work.

6. Make sure there is no surplus of fabric at the back which might be caught in the stitchery.

OPPOSITE
*Work in progress: **Calyx**, by Tryphena Orchard.*
The fabric is mounted on a slate frame. The design was tacked on to the fabric through tracing paper and the outline can be seen on the unworked area. Materials used for the embroidery include beads, sequin waste, padded and quilted gold kid, purls and metal threads.

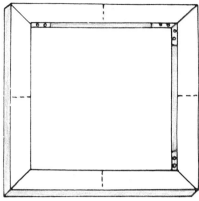

A home-made frame.

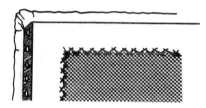

A corner of a home-made frame (or old picture frame) showing the backing fabric stretched on the frame with drawing pins, and the top fabric laid over and sewn in place with herringbone stitch.

Ring frame

This should only be used for a small design which is totally contained within the ring. Ring frames are not generally recommended for goldwork as the fabric will have to be continually adjusted to keep it taut. Always use one with a stand, so that both hands are free.

1. Bind the inner ring with tape to prevent the fabric slipping.

2. Lay the fabric over the inner ring, then press the outer ring into place.

3. Stretch and tension the fabric, then tighten the screw.

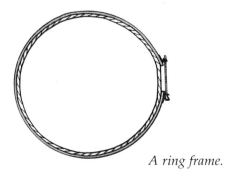

A ring frame.

Transferring the design to the fabric

Trace-and-tack method

This is one of the simplest ways of transferring a design. Trace the design on to tracing or greaseproof paper, place it on the fabric in the frame, and then tack through the outline, using a sewing thread in a contrasting colour. The top stitches should be longer than the underneath ones. When this is done, scratch along the lines with a pin to tear the paper, which will then lift away. An advantage of this method is that, if you change your mind as you work, the lines are not permanent.

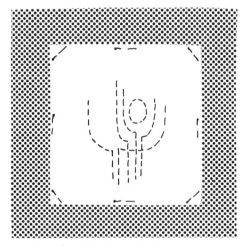

Trace-and-tack method.

Template method

This is suitable for simple outlines and repeating patterns. Trace off the shape, then paste the tracing on to thin card and cut it out. Lay the resulting template in position on the framed fabric and mark round it with chalk, washable embroidery pencil or a fine hard pencil. Alternatively, the shape can be outlined with fine running stitches.

Transfer paper

This method is not suitable for rough or textured fabrics, and might be difficult to erase if the design ideas were changed during the progress of the work. Use dressmaking carbon paper. Place it shiny side down on the fabric and cover with the traced design. Position and secure with pins or masking tape. Go over the lines of the design with a fine hard pencil. Check that the design is transferred satisfactorily before lifting off the carbon and the tracing.

***Aztec Indian Head**, by Sylvia Drinkwater, using padded kid and a variety of couched braids, beads, gold threads, silks and sequin waste. Three layers of net accentuate the face, while the curtaining fabric design echoes the subject.*

Padding

Padding is often used with metal threads as it increases the play of light on them, and the taut, framed fabric supports the raised areas. It is not a good idea to work too much padding on clothes or vestments, as it tends to look too heavy and solid, and makes odd bumps on the body.

Felt

The area to be padded is marked on a piece of felt and is cut out. Another piece is cut out in a slightly smaller size of the same shape, and then a third piece even smaller. The smallest piece is then sewn or glued in the middle of the area to be padded, then the middle-sized piece over it, and finally the largest. This results in a dome-shaped area of padding which can be covered with threads, wires, fabric or leather.

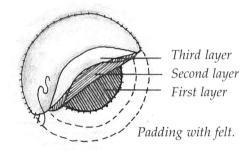

Third layer
Second layer
First layer

Padding with felt.

Applying leather over padding

Gold and silver kid is usually applied over padding. Having sewn down the felt layers, tack the leather in place by taking the stitches right over the shape and not through it, to avoid extra holes. Sew down with small straight stitches round the edge – the stitch comes up through the background fabric and goes down through the leather.

Applying leather.

Card

Small pieces of card can be used as padding and give a firmer line than felt. Paint the card with coloured ink so that it is unobtrusive, and then sew it to the ground with a few stitches. All these forms of padding can be covered with couched threads.

Card used as padding.

Trapunto quilting

Small areas of a design can be stuffed from the back and made to stand out from a design.

The fabric should be soft and pliable, and should be mounted on a firm backing which will allow the top fabric to plump up, otherwise the padded effect may appear underneath instead of on top. Keep the shapes simple and small. Work a close back-stitch around the area to be raised. Make a tiny slit in the back and stuff with lambswool or synthetic wadding (do not use cotton wool as it tends to become lumpy). Push it in with an orange stick or scissor points until the shape is well filled, and then stitch up the slit.

Stages of working trapunto quilting:

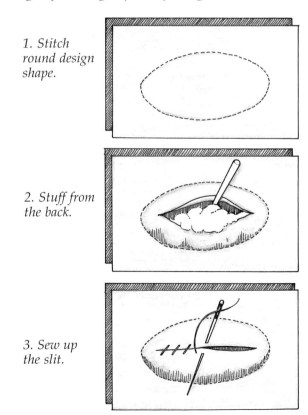

1. Stitch round design shape.

2. Stuff from the back.

3. Sew up the slit.

Beetle: *a panel by Angela Thompson embroidered in padded gold kid and couched metal threads and purls on a green slubbed-silk background.*

Couching metal threads

Couching is a method of securing decorative ornamental threads to the ground material by means of a different and normally finer 'working thread'. The ends of couched metal thread are left free and are taken to the 'wrong' side of the work only after sewing is completed in order to avoid a tangle at the back, so leave 2.5–5cm (1–2in) unused at the beginning.

The couching stitches can be worked in a matching or contrasting colour.

Thread a needle with the appropriate colour of sewing thread, run it through the beeswax, and make a knot. Bring it up through the fabric at the beginning of a line and take a small stitch over the metal thread at right angles to it. Hold the metal thread firmly (or two together if they are fine) and pull very slightly as you work. Continue with stitches about 4mm (¼in) apart, but closer together around the curves.

At the end of the line finish off the sewing thread with a back-stitch underneath a future area of embroidery. Cut off the metal thread, leaving a short length hanging. When the work is finished, thread the end into a chenille needle and take it through to the back of the work. Oversew it in place under an area already embroidered in order to avoid a lump showing on the surface. Adhesive tape can be used to hold the ends in place at the back.

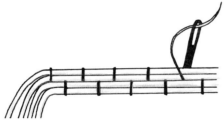

The start: the ends of couched lines of doubled threads are left hanging, to be taken through to the back later.

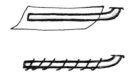

The finish: the ends of metal threads taken through to the back are held in place with adhesive tape or with overcasting.

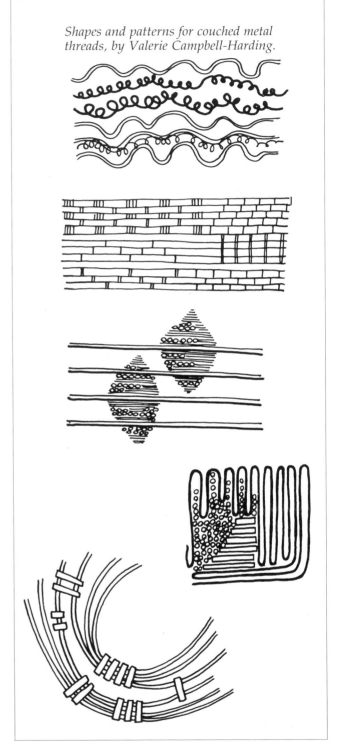

Shapes and patterns for couched metal threads, by Valerie Campbell-Harding.

OPPOSITE
Sample of couched metal threads, by Valerie Campbell-Harding: several kinds of purl and Jap gold couched on to a silk background.

To fill a shape with couching

When you fill in a shape such as a circle, a rounded square, or a free shape, always start at the outside and work towards the centre to make sure that the shape is accurate. This is impossible to do if you start in the centre. If you are working with two threads together, start them in different places about 12mm (¹/₂in) apart to avoid a lump. Wavy lines can be couched in different patterns to accentuate the play of light. Where the lines change direction, the threads can be spaced out.

A couched circle, showing the double thread starting at different points to make a smooth edge.

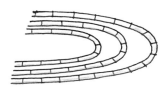

An easy method of changing direction with the threads, which can leave fabric showing through the spaces.

To turn corners

When working sharp corners, you should make an extra stitch at the corner at a 45-degree angle to hold the metal thread in place. If you are working with two threads together, the outer thread is secured first, followed by the inner one with a separate stitch. Try to keep the spacing of the other stitching as regular as possible.

A right-angled corner, with two separate stitches in each thread at the corner to keep the angle sharp.

To turn threads sharply

When you work a solid area of couching, the threads must be turned back on themselves with no spaces showing. With a single thread this is fairly easy, as a stitch is put at the end of the row, the thread pulled back on itself, and a stitch worked over the double thread to hold them together. When you are working with two threads, the outer thread is secured with a stitch, then the inner one, then both threads are pulled back against themselves and a stitch worked over both threads. Now continue couching as normally.

Another method, when working with pairs of threads, is to cut off one of the threads, turn the other thread, and start a new one alongside it. This method can weaken the fabric, so be careful how many ends go through it too near to each other.

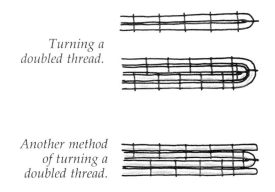

Turning a doubled thread.

Another method of turning a doubled thread.

To make sharp angles

When several threads are couched together and have to turn at a sharp angle, there is only one way to keep the point sharp. The outermost thread is cut and taken round the point, but each succeeding thread is cut and taken through to the back, alternately from side to side, so that they dovetail.

A sharp point with multiple couched threads.

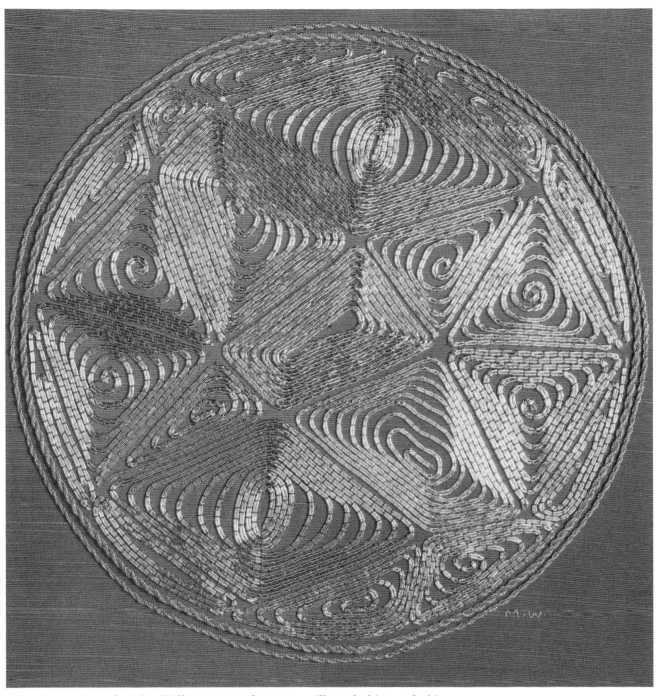

Circular pattern, by May Williams: a panel on green silk worked in couched Jap gold, the patterns of which throw up charming reflections according to the light.

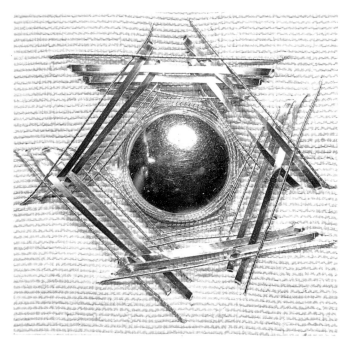

Free use of plate, by Valerie Campbell-Harding: plate used to outline a central metal boss.

Couched plate (part of burse on page 43), by Heidi Jenkins: plate decoratively couched in a square surrounding a mass of tiny beads.

To sew plate

Fold back a tiny piece at the beginning of the length to form a hook, and then secure this to the fabric with two stitches. The plate is then folded backwards and forwards, either flat or over string, and each fold is secured with a stitch. At the end another hook is made.

Sewing down plate.

To apply cord

Some flat braids can be sewn down the centre. Twisted cords should be sewn with an angled stitch which slips between the twists and becomes invisible.

Sewing down Russia braid.

Sewing a twisted cord.

String

This may be sewn in spaced rows for a filling to be covered by couched threads, or in a single line to be covered by plate or purls. Secure the string to the fabric with two stitches near one end, going through the centre of the string. Then sew along the length with alternate stitches each side going through the string, pulling slightly as you work. Bring the sewing thread up through the fabric and down into the string.

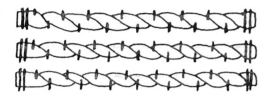

String sewn in place.

Couching over string

When you sew metal threads over string, make a double stitch over the metal thread close to the string.

In basket pattern the gold thread is passed over two strings, and the thread is then couched close to the side of the second string with a double stitch. Flat areas between the raised areas are sewn with the usual couching patterns.

Basket work is very rich, but it is too stiff to be worn and should be kept for panels, boxes or book covers, purses, and other flat articles.

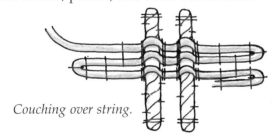

Couching over string.

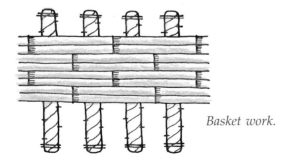

Basket work.

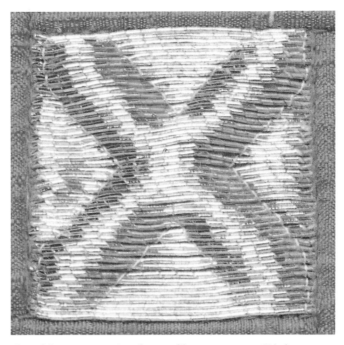

Couching over string (part of burse on page 43), *by Heidi Jenkins. A St Andrew's cross reflects the light from the raised outline.*

Letter M, by Valerie Campbell-Harding: couched cords, plate and silk threads on a cream twill background.

Kodak Advanced Photos
FEB/8/04   ID263-677   <39>   KBW46

OPPOSITE
Pulled-thread work with gold threads: sample, *by*
Eileen Plumbridge.This design is based on cordon trees
and executed in pulled-thread work technique using a
thin gold passing thread, together with couched Jap gold,
and other gold threads.

BELOW
Letter S panel, *by May Williams. The letter shape is*
filled with sweeping lines of couched Jap gold expanding
at each end round a circle packed with tightly
embroidered tiny flowers, while the inner pieces are filled
with padded gold kid. A tiny repetition of the design is
used as a full stop.

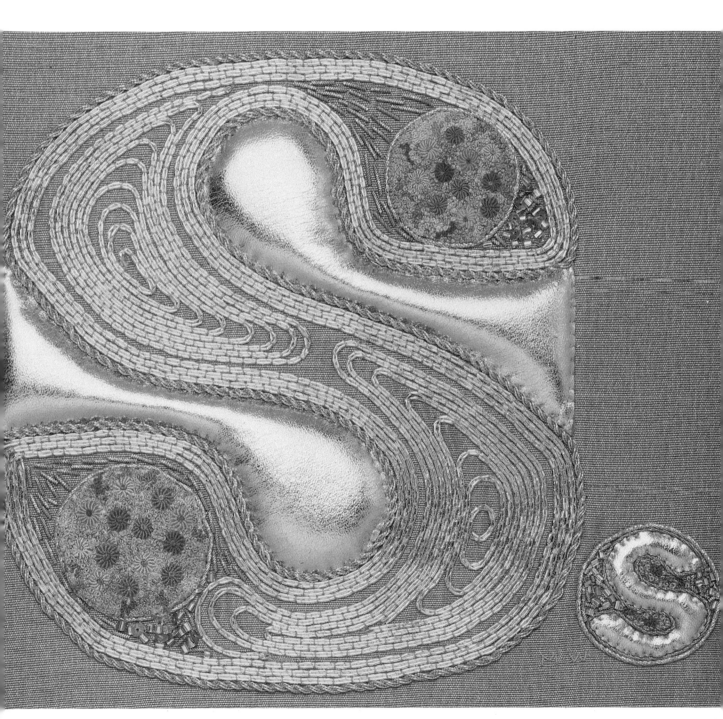

Or nué

Or nué is the stitching of metal threads with a fine coloured thread to make shaded or coloured patterns. The gold threads cover the whole surface of the design (or an area within a design) and the spacing of the coloured stitching is varied to show more or less gold. It is extremely rich and beautiful, although rather slow to work.

Historical use

Or nué was worked in England in the Middle Ages and up to the middle of the seventeenth century. The designs were realistic and usually on ecclesiastical vestments. Often the shading was used to show folds of fabric on figures of saints and apostles.

Designing for or nué

Designs can be realistic or abstract, geometric or based on natural forms. They should be fairly simple shapes without too much detail. It is advisable to make a coloured sketch drawing, using gold poster paint with coloured poster paint on top. Trace the design and transfer the lines to a fabric backing, which must be fairly strong to support the heavy gold. It might be helpful to paint the coloured areas on the backing with thinned fabric paints.

Method

Take two smooth gold threads and a needle threaded with gold-coloured sewing thread. Start at the bottom right-hand corner, leaving 7.5cm (3in) of the gold threads hanging to be finished off later.

Couch the gold threads along the bottom edge of the design until a coloured area is reached. Leave the sewing thread on the surface of the work ready for the next row. Thread another needle with the desired colour and couch the gold threads with it. The stitches can be 6mm (¼in) apart, or as close together as possible, in order completely to cover the gold, according to the design. The stitches should be worked at right angles to the gold threads and in a brick pattern if possible.

When you reach the next coloured area, leave the first thread for the next row, thread up the new colour and work the next area with it. Continue like this until the left-hand side of the line is reached, with a new thread for each colour. The gold threads are turned and each coloured thread in succession is picked up to couch them.

Do not use too many colours until you have gained some experience. Work gradually up the design, completely covering the background fabric.

Finish off the gold threads in the usual way after taking them through to the back of the work.

Variations in working or nué

Although the method just described is the most usual one, there are certain variations which will give a more modern look:

1. The lines of gold need not be horizontal, but can follow the contour of a shape.

2. *Or nué* can be used in small areas of a design, or combined with other goldwork, hand or machine stitchery, or counted-thread work.

3. Silver threads, gold and silver threads, or metal and coloured threads together can be used instead of gold alone.

4. The metal threads could be cords or textured threads, combined with smooth ones for contrast.

5. Padding can be used to raise some of the shapes between coloured stitching. The couching is worked only on the flat areas between the padding.

OPPOSITE

Canvas-work with or nué: *frame for an icon photograph, by Jean Brown. The object was to achieve a rich but sympathetic frame for the icon. The postcard-sized photograph was attached to 14-mesh canvas which was then worked in a variety of threads. The main part of the frame is in* or-nué *technique, with horizontal and vertical rows of gold thread (a double thread of gold for each line of the canvas). The patterns were worked over the gold in a synthetic white and gold knitting yarn and a pale-yellow knitting wool. Sequin waste is incorporated into the canvas-work around the inner edge of the frame.*

Or nué, *by Valerie Campbell-Harding.*

ABOVE
The working drawing.

RIGHT
The work in progress, showing the felt padding in place, and the different coloured threads being used for couching so as to form a coloured pattern on the lines of couched gold thread.

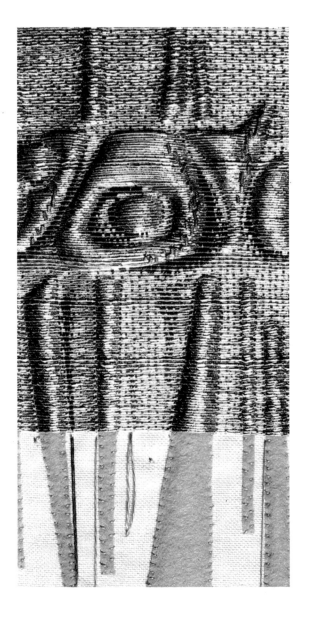

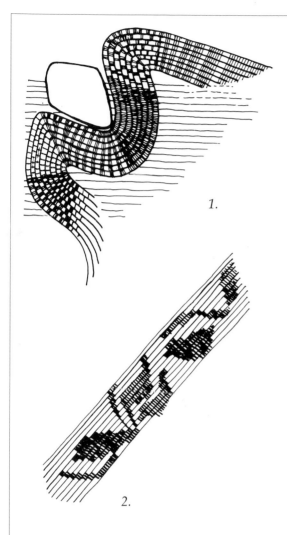

1.

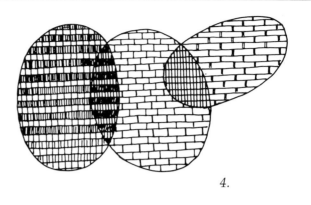

4.

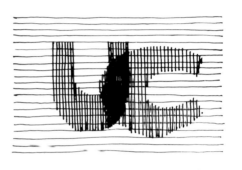

5.

2.

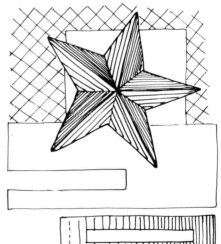

3.

Ideas for the use of or nué, by Valerie Campbell-Harding.

1. Lines following a shape and areas of colour.

2 and 3. Gold threads sewn with regular patterns in colour.

4 and 5. Overlapped shapes.

6. Traditional couched star, but with colour on one side of each point for a three-dimensional effect.

6.

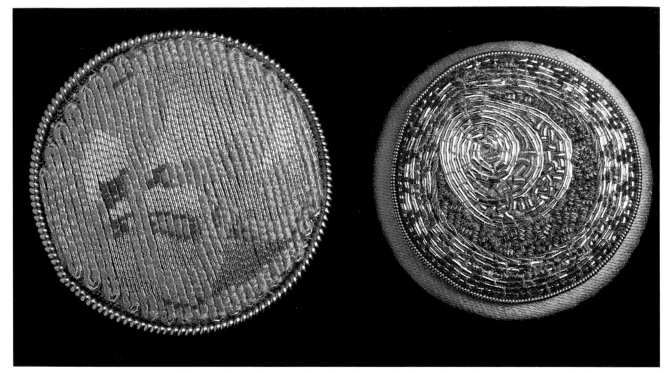

Goldwork buttons *by Jennie Parry.*

LEFT

This design, worked in or nué, was taken from an Art Nouveau brass button. Double gold thread was couched with two strands of silk in two shades, darker for the shadows. Two No. 10 crewel needles were used, one for each block of stitching. The button is edged with purl wire No. 2.

RIGHT

Couched gold thread and purls worked on cotton string, with imitation Jap, coloured silk threads and a variety of check, smooth and rough purl, outlined in very fine purl wire. The designs were worked to fit 4cm (1½in) commercial button moulds. The fabric and backing were stretched in a frame. When completed and taken off the frame, the work was trimmed as indicated in the instructions. A gathering thread was run around the edge of the circle, the button centred behind the embroidery and the thread drawn up. The fabric was eased round and the ends of the thread fastened off before the back plate was snapped on.

Sewing purls

Purls are made of finely drawn wire coiled tightly like a spring. There are so many sizes and textures of purl, and they are so easy to use, that they are an essential part of metal-thread embroidery.

Purls can be cut into short lengths and threaded on a needle to be sewn like a bead. Purls can be used as a powdering over an area, as geometric patterns and fillings, or over padded areas.

Cut the lengths on the cutting board, to keep them together, using tough nail-scissors held at right angles to the wire. The lengths are not usually longer than 12mm (¹/₂in).

Pearl purl is much heavier, and this is couched with the sewing thread slipping between the coils so that it does not show. Pearl purl can be used as a continuous length – it is usually stretched slightly to enable the sewing thread to slip into the coil and to remove kinks. For decorative effect it may be stretched even more. It will bend easily, and turn very sharp corners to make accurate lines. The ends are left on the surface, so that none is wasted.

Care should be taken when deciding whether or not to use purls on a garment. Since the ends tend to catch and pull in wear, they are often impractical.

Sewing cut purl.

Covering string with purl.

Ideas for using purl, by Valerie Campbell-Harding.

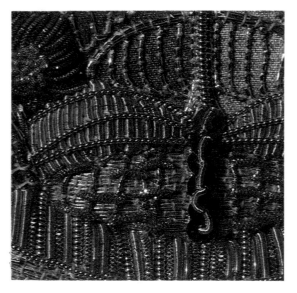

Close-up of buckle on page 36,
by Elizabeth Elvin.

Couched pearl purl,
by Valerie Campbell-Harding.

Couched check purl *(part of burse on page 43),*
by Heidi Jenkins: check purl and New Jap gold
couched with green sewing silk.

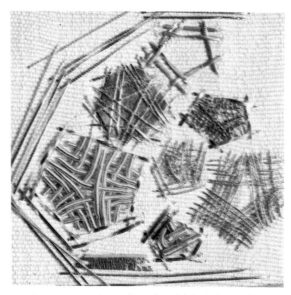

Purl, passing thread and gold kid, *by Valerie*
Campbell-Harding. Different materials are used
to vary the texture of repeated shapes.

Purls and straight stitch: drawstring bag.
*A traditional rose-spray design was marked in regular parallel lines,
which were worked alternately in cut purl and thick silk thread.
Different shades of silk were used, with check purl for the flowers,
smooth purl for the leaves, and pearl purl for the ribbon.*

Decorative buckle, *by Elizabeth Elvin: an experimental piece which was worked in a ring frame with a double calico backing. The padding consists of string, and carpet felt covered with thinner felt. All kinds of metal thread are used for the embroidery, including some tarnished check purl for the deeper tones.*

Patchwork evening bag, by Jean Panter: patchwork in three shades of silk-and-wool-mixture fabric, with gold purls worked on some of the flap sections, finished with a hand-made cord.

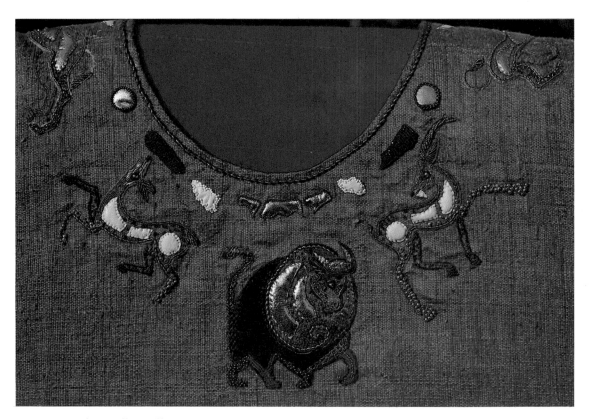

Waistcoat, by Mollie Collins. A circle of animal designs around the neckline of a Thai silk waistcoat is worked in appliquéd fabric and padded gold kid, with beads and metal-thread embroidery.

Church embroidery

Since the establishment of Christianity in Britain, every generation has contributed to the building, decoration and care of British churches and cathedrals. This tradition continues today through our artists and musicians, poets and writers, and craftsmen and embroiderers.

Designing for the Church

Design is all-important where embroidery is concerned. There is naturally a great deal of earlier work still in use, and because the general public has grown up with it it is considered by many parochial church councils to be the type of design best suited to their church, whatever the period in which it was built. What is sometimes forgotten is that this embroidery was modern in its own time, and that work from our own period can be used in the same way.

Work for the Church is not just a decoration but is an expression of belief, with the purpose of inspiring the congregation to deeper thought. The design should be unique and personal to the proposed building with the theme arising from within; perhaps an architectural detail, a stained-glass window, the symbol of the saint to whom the church is dedicated, or some historic event of the locality. The design should combine with the whole interior setting, making a unified and satisfying visual whole.

The movement of line within the architecture and that within the embroidery must be in harmony. It is important to aim at this quality of movement and energy, especially in altar frontals in the larger churches and cathedrals, to draw the eye to the focal point. It is also helpful to the congregation if the design allows the eye to travel happily over it in a satisfying manner.

Although the design should be clear from the furthest point of a building, it must have the subtlety to arouse interest as it is approached. This means that strength of line is needed, plus plenty of details which can be enjoyed when closely examined.

Variation of tone is vital, as a change of colour alone will not allow the design to be seen from afar. If the tone values of two important design areas do not vary sufficiently to show the line as the design requires, there are several methods that can be used to accentuate it. One of the areas may be padded and raised to create a shadow along the line, or the line may be strengthened by laying a darker hand-made cord along the edge – this is not to recommend that shapes are outlined, but to help a design be visible from a distance – and it may not be noticeable until the frontal is viewed from the sanctuary steps. If more strength is needed, try texturing on the unpadded section of the design, to build up the depth of the shadow. This can be done with machine stitching, running stitches, French knots or similar stitchery.

Three-dimensional cross, by Heidi Jenkins: *made of gold kid stretched over a base of cotton rope padded with felt. Beads provide the diagonal decorations.*

It is a temptation to have too much of a theatrical approach, and to assume that the view from a distance is all-important. This can result in the use of cheap fabrics and threads, and however good the design these do not do justice to a place of worship. With the rise in the cost of commissions and materials, the temptation is very understandable, but the finished results when using quality materials not only look far better, but will also stand the test of time better.

Colours must be selected in the building, and in the actual area where they will be used. The variations of light, and the result of the light's being reflected off the stone, change the colours appreciably – apart from the intensity of light being reduced. Very often, when the colour patterns are checked in the daylight, they look too strong, but you should stand by the decision you took in the church, even if it means returning there to confirm your choice.

The use of colour in the church is being more appreciated these days, as can be seen by the reintroduction of painted ceilings and organ pipes and the restoration of areas that originally were painted. Liturgical colours do have slight variations in their adoption, depending on which Cathedral Use is followed, but even these are being allowed a wider interpretation in order to suit the area or background that will incorporate the embroidery.

Consider the colour of the stone or brick when you select fabrics for vestments. Many a beautiful white, cream or pale-yellow cope or chasuble disappears into the background when in use in the church! This applies especially to large buildings where the priest needs to be visible from far back in the nave. Care must be taken, too, in selecting the pattern from which to cut the vestment, so that it both fits the wearer and suits his environment.

Fabrics should be chosen to stand up to the wear and tear demanded of the article. A textural quality gives a lively start, but all depends on the overall design. Use good-quality backing or interlining, not only to hold the embroidery but also to give substance and quality to the work. Choose metallised fabrics with great care, as some of them catch and snag easily and a vestment incorporating them can soon look shoddy.

Fabrics selected for vestments should hang well and be thoroughly tested for creasing. Linen is very crushable and difficult to look after in the vestry, whereas pure wool loses its creases very quickly. Pure silk has a beauty and life of its own and is well worth the expense: it comes in so many weights and finishes that one can surely be found to fit every purpose, and the depth of colour is most rewarding.

Care must be taken with the choice of threads and techniques for vestments, as they must not be liable to catch on anything when folded or worn. See that the weight of the garment is well balanced, and that it is not heavy or uncomfortable to wear.

The following pages show a recently designed frontal for Salisbury Cathedral and a chasuble for a village church. You can follow the progress of the frontal design from commission to making up.

Page from a designer's sketchbook, by Jane Lemon.

All Saints' Church, Steeple Langford.

Carved wooden motifs taken from the pulpit and Rector's stall – made from the original Jacobean three-decker pulpit dated 1613.

'Energy' frontal from Salisbury Cathedral, by Jane Lemon and members of the Sarum Group of the Embroiderers' Guild. (Photograph by Sam Kelly, by permission of the Dean and Chapter.)

The 'Energy' Frontal, Salisbury Cathedral

The commission given to Jane Lemon and the Sarum Group of the Embroiderers' Guild was to design and make an all-seasons high-altar frontal to link with the new east window.

The Sarum rite states that the frontal should be red, not the more usual green, but it was essential to use some blue to draw the window into the sanctuary and to make it a visual whole with the altar.

The movement and colour in the design represent a living faith and the energy that is required to live as a practising Christian.

The design of the chalice was taken from one discovered in a tomb under repair, and it was worked in *or nué* and leather. Padded, it stands out from the background by nearly 2.5cm (1in).

A solid rose thorn was chosen instead of the needle-type blackthorn, as the design needed to be very clear because of the great length of the nave. The design was first presented to the Dean as a scale-model cardboard cut-out at a scale of 2.5cm = 30cm (1in = 1ft) to see if he approved of the general scheme and colouring. Once the Dean's approval was obtained, the design was enlarged on to a good strong paper which formed the base on which coloured paper could be pinned and glued to make a full-size mock-up. The paper mock-up was then presented to the Dean and Chapter and was pinned up in position on the high altar for general review.

It takes a great deal of table or floor space to assemble the full-scale design! Space is also required for the frame on which the fabric is mounted, and it is far more satisfactory to keep these large frontals on a permanent frame, which carries the weight and holds them taut, than to hang or roll them. When the work is finished, it can be stored without folding and when in use it can be attached by a touch-and-close (hook-and-loop) fabric such as Velcro to a throw-over cloth, made to fit the altar.

The permanent frame is mounted with linen or a good heavy calico using upholstery methods. You should not drive tacks home, or neaten the back, as the linen or calico will need to be retightened before the work is finally completed.

The chalice, and the crown of thorns divided into three sections, were worked separately on four slate frames and then applied to the permanent frame when the background was completed. The crown of thorns was worked in padded, manipulated and piped leathers of different colours and tones. The textural quality makes a strong contrast to the smoothness of the chalice.

When working in a 'theatrical' setting, it is often helpful to use a different technique for the appliqué, instead of the usual flat application. Each piece of fabric is cut with a 2.5cm (1in) turning and bonded on to the pelmet interfacing cut to the accurate shape. In some designs, additional layers of felt may be tacked to the interfacing to give more height.

On the *Energy* frontal the pale area behind the chalice was completely flat, then each following fabric shape was mounted on pelmet interfacing and lapped one on to another to give a progressively more raised effect towards the outside edges of the frontal. This meant that the turnings of the silk were turned back behind the interfacing on the inside edge of each swirl (and secured with herringbone stitch to give a clean, sharp finish) and the silk was left flat with a turning allowance on the interfacing of about 6cm (2½in) on the outside edge of the swirls. This allowed the next colour to be laid over the first and subsequently raised.

Obviously, the smaller pieces which lie completely on top of a single colour have to have the interfacing cut to shape and the turning of the silk herringboned back all the way round. The silk-covered interfacing shapes are applied to the framed frontal with ladder stitch, using a curved needle where necessary.

This method gives a slight shadow on the edges of each colour, which gives depth to the design. It also means that any machine or hand embroidery can be worked on each prepared piece before it is applied to the frame.

It is possible to use as many embroiderers as the design allows, using separate frames. The Lenten frontal in Salisbury Cathedral had thirteen people working the pulled- and drawn-thread pieces. It is important, however, to have one person directing the work and having an overall picture of the resulting embroidery, otherwise the result could be unbalanced.

It is possible to use up to four people sewing on the permanent frame if time is of the essence, but two or three is really more comfortable. Working together in a group can be rewarding – and fun.

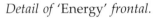

Detail of 'Energy' *frontal.*

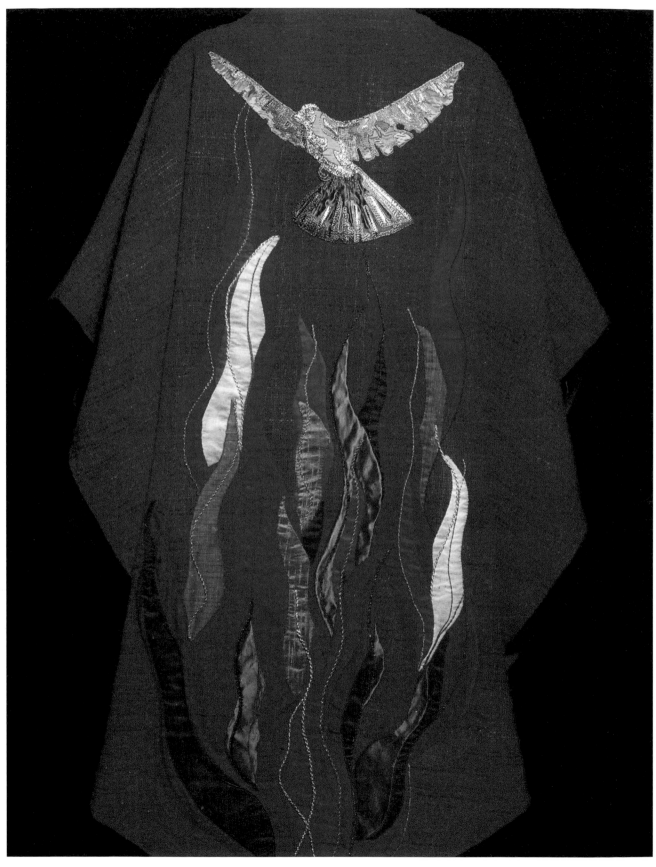

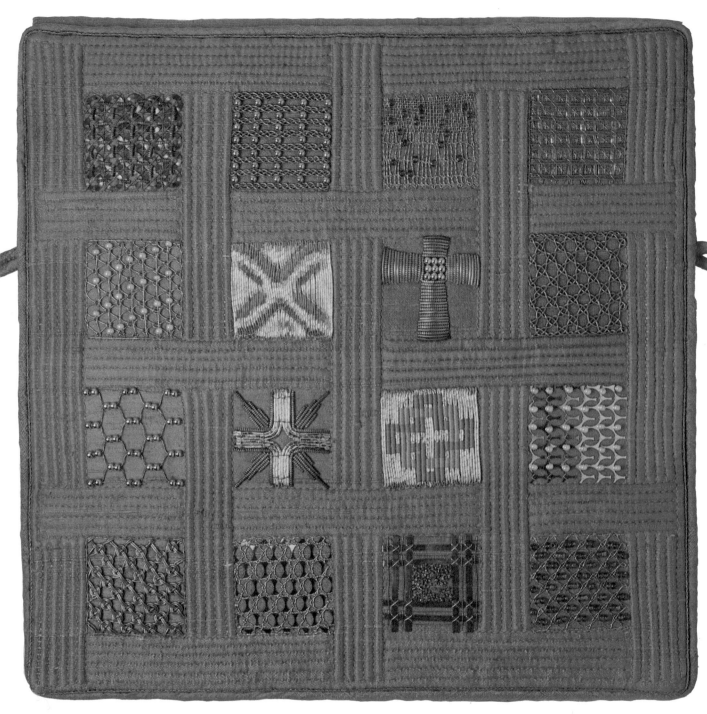

LEFT
Chasuble, by Jane Lemon for St Mary's Church, Wylye,
Wiltshire.

ABOVE
Burse by Heidi Jenkins: metal-thread embroidery on
green shot silk.

The four designs in the centre show traditional goldwork
techniques on four different cross designs:

1. Raised shape covered with couching in New Jap gold.

2. Cut lengths of bright purl and check purl with bead
centre.

3. Check purl and New Jap gold couched with green
sewing silk.

4. Or nué technique in two tones of green.

Some of the outer squares make use of sequin waste, gold
plate bands, brass washers, beads, pearls and purl grit
(tiny pieces of purl). Others are filled with needle-lace
stitches using a variety of metal threads.

Jewels, glass, beads and stones

'Jewels', in embroidery, are generally cut faceted pieces of coloured glass, with one or more holes pierced near the edge so you can secure them to the fabric. They are often attached in decorative ways, with surrounding stitchery to conceal the stitches through the holes.

1. Basic method of attaching a jewel, with stitches through the holes.

2. The stitches through the holes are threaded with cut purl, and the jewel is edged with tiny beads.

3–6. Jewels held in place with stitches through the holes and then surrounded with cut purl or metal threads.

Polished stones are often used with metal-thread embroidery, and also other objects such as shavings of mother-of-pearl, shells, coins, lumps of glass, pebbles and slices of wood, none of which have holes for stitching. These can be attached by adhesive, by covering the object with a net of stitchery such as needle-weaving, or by embedding them in leather or non-woven fabric.

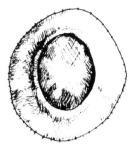

Applied leather ring over stone.

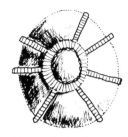

Buttonhole ring with radiating bars.

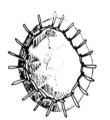

Buttonhole edge.

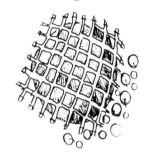

Lurex mesh over stone and beads.

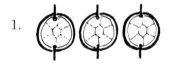

1. *Ideas for securing jewels and stones.*

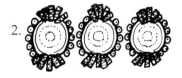

2.

3. 4.

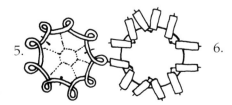

5. 6.

Ways of attaching beads

1. Beads can be secured by a single stitch through the hole.

2. A tiny bead in the centre of a large one stops the thread pulling through.

3. A pile of small beads can be anchored with three threads through the centre spaced round the pile.

4. To make short hanging lengths of beads, take a stitch through the final one and then pass the needle back again through the others.

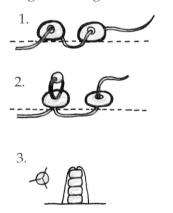

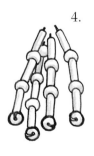

1.

2.

3.

4.

Egrets, *by Sylvia Drinkwater: a panel using couched threads and various beads and braids on a silk background with a gold-painted sun.*

Goldwork with appliqué and beads: pole screen, by Diana Gill. This design is based on
a scabious flower, and is worked on deep-turquoise shot silk in couched gold and silver thread
of many varieties. Leather and beads add texture and highlights, and the background is
further shaded by massed bullion knots worked in shades of stranded silk.

Finishing your work

While the embroidery is still in the frame, take all the ends through to the back and secure them. Then remove the embroidery from the frame. If you are mounting your work, cut out a piece of hardboard (for large pieces) or thick card (for small ones) to size, and cover it with a piece of thin wadding which is slightly larger all round.

Fold the excess over to the back and secure it with adhesive tape, trimming away all the bulk at the corners. Next, cut any spare backing fabric away from the embroidery to avoid bulk and place the work upside down on a piece of tissue paper on a table. Place the card or board on top of it.

Turn the whole thing over and centre the embroidery on the board. Pin into the edge of the board all round to hold the embroidery in place.

Turn the work upside down again and lace the fabric across the back with crochet cotton. Leave the cotton on the ball and draw off thread as required while you are lacing.

Finish off one end when you reach an edge, tighten it back to the beginning and finish that off. Turn the board round and lace in the other direction. Finally, remove the pins.

This is not necessary for a garment or vestment, which is made up in the usual way.

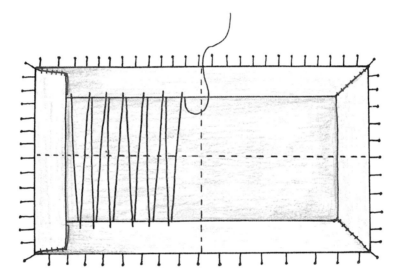

Lacing the back of a panel.

Index

Set of burse, veil and stole matching the chasuble on page 42, by Jane Lemon for St Mary's Church, Wylye.